COFFEE & HOLIDAY
MIXOLOGY

32 Iconic Bars Share Their Signature Themed Cocktails

BY
STEVE AKLEY

Written and Published by:
Steve Akley

Text copyright © 2016 Steve Akley
All Rights Reserved

Cover Design © 2016 Mark Hansen
All Rights Reserved

To People Who Love Coffee, the Holidays and Cocktails:

These are a few of my favorite things!

Coffee & Holiday Mixology
32 Iconic Bars Share Their Signature Themed Cocktails

Introduction by Steve Akley, Author

With the success of my first two **Bourbon Mixology** books, and a third being released the same time as this offering, I thought I would expand my horizons a bit. My idea was to look at other types of cocktails besides bourbon-based drinks. My idea for this book was to feature two unique types of mixed drinks that would be of great interest. I would present them in one book, but separate them like they are two books within one.

The first themed cocktails we explore are coffee-based. While coffee may dominate drink consumption in the a.m. hours, it appears to me that it is grossly underappreciated in the p.m. **Coffee Mixology** explores cocktails made with everyone's favorite caffeinated beverage.

The second part of the book, **Holiday Mixology**, explores cocktails with a holiday theme. Whether they have a name that ties directly to a specific holiday, or, they are simply beverages like spiced mulled cider that are typically enjoyed during the holidays, I've put together some great cocktails you will want to showcase at your festive parties this year.

With the last edition of **Bourbon Mixology** I started a tradition of including one additional cocktail beyond what is on the cover. With this being two books in one, I actually have included one extra recipe in each of the books within a book. These bonus recipes come from 18.21 Bitters. I actually had contacted them accidentally thinking they were a bar. Alas, they were not. They sell ingredients to make cocktails. Since they did respond with such great cocktails, and I have this policy of giving readers of this series "more than promised," I decided to include them as the bonus cocktail recipes.

Another component to this publication is the iconic bars themselves. You will certainly want to use these books as a travel companion. Seek out these iconic venues in your travels. There isn't a better way to enjoy the drinks you see here than having them mixed up by the people who actually created them.

Enjoy this fun look at coffee and holiday-themed cocktails!

Table of Contents

Coffee Mixology 8
   The Brooklynite 9
   Buffalo Proper 11
   Coffee House Cafe 13
   Dandelion Market 15
   Elixir 17
   Establishment 19
   Full Throttle Saloon 21
   The Honeymoon 23
   Mr. C's Irish Pub 25
   Piastra 27
   The Red Rabbit Kitchen and Bar 29
   The Roosevelt Room 31
   Spenard Roadhouse 33
   Talbott Tavern 35
   Tavern Law 37
   The Third Man 39
   Trenchermen 41
   Vanguard Lounge 43
   The Way Station 45
   Bonus Coffee Cocktail: Saints+Sinners 47

Holiday Mixology 49
   40 Steak and Seafood 50
   116 Crown 52
   Boiler Room 54
   Butch McGuire's 56

Cardinal Tavern	58
Dickie Brennan's Steakhouse	60
Herbie's Vintage 72	62
Novela	64
The Royal Mile	66
Sloppy Joe's	69
Supply and Demand	71
Urban Tree Cidery	73
Whiskey Bar	75
Bonus Holiday Cocktail: The Bitter Grinch	77
Author's Notes/Resources	79
Steve's Other Works	84
Special Thanks	85
Love A Cat Charity – Honolulu, Hawai'i	86
About the Author	87
Find Steve on Social Media	87
Bourbon Zeppelin	87

The Brooklynite

516 Brooklyn Avenue
San Antonio, TX 78215
(210) 444-0707

brooklynitesa.com
info@brooklynite.com

Established
2012

Leadership
Jeret Peña

The Rosella

Submitted by: Jeret Peña, The Broolynite

Serve in a martini glass:
- 1 ½ ounces rye whiskey
- ¾ ounce Carpano Antic Vermouth infused with Rosella Coffee (medium roast)
- ¼ ounce saffron syrup
- Orange zest
1. Pour all ingredients in martini glass
2. Stir
3. Add orange zest and serve

Buffalo Proper

333 Franklin Street
Buffalo, NY 14202
(716) 783-8699

buffaloproper.com

Established
2014

Leadership
Jon Karel, Edward Forster, Josh Miles & Tyler Wolk

Casltebar

Submitted by: Jon Karel, Buffalo Proper

Serve in an Irish coffee mug:
- 1 ounce Powers Gold Irish Whisky
- ¼ ounce Fernet Branca
- ¼ ounce simple syrup
- 4 ounces coffee (205 degrees, not quite boiling)
- 1 ounce heavy cream (36% fat)
- Fresh grated nutmeg
1. Build first 3 ingredients in traditional Irish coffee glass
2. Add coffee
3. Float cream
4. Grate nutmeg on top

Coffee House Cafe

6150 Frankford Road
Dallas, TX 75252
(972) 232-2287

coffeehousecafe.com
info@coffeehousecafe.com

Established
2010

Leadership
Carrie Kelleher

Coffee House Cafe Irish Latte

Submitted by: Heather Carmichael, Coffee House Cafe

Serve in a latte mug:
- ¾ ounce Jameson's Irish Whiskey
- ¾ ounce Bailey's Irish Cream
- 1 shot espresso
- Frothed milk
- Whipped cream
- Crème de Menth

1. In a standard latte cup, combine Jameson's, Bailey's and the shot of espresso
2. Froth milk and pour into mixture, leaving room for whipped cream
3. Top with whipped cream and garnish with a thin drizzle of dark Crème de Menthe
4. Optional garnish: dark Crème de Menthe on ⅓ and Crème de Cassis on the opposite ⅓ to create an Irish flag

Dandelion Market

118 West 5th Street
Charlotte, NC 28202
(704) 333-7989

dandelionmarketcharlotte.com
info@thedandelionmarket.com

Established
2009

Leadership
Tommy Timmins, Kevin Devin & Maynard Goble

The Last Word

Submitted by: Brian Woulfe, Dandelion Market

Serve in a rocks glass:
- 1 ½ ounces espresso infused bourbon
- Ice
- Orange zest
1. In a cocktail shaker, combine ice and espresso infused bourbon
2. Shake well
3. Fill a whiskey glass with fresh ice and strain the bourbon over it
4. Garnish with an orange zest

Espresso Infused Bourbon Recipe
- 1 cup Bulleit Bourbon
- ⅛ cup Grand Marnier
- ⅛ cup Antica Sweet Vermouth
- ¼ cup dark roast espresso beans
- ⅛ cup water
- ⅛ cup dark brown sugar
- 1 vanilla bean
- Zest from 1 orange
1. Scrape the seeds from the inside of the vanilla bean and combine with water and dark brown sugar
2. Heat just until the sugar is melted to create a simple syrup
3. Combine the simple syrup with all other ingredients
4. Shake or stir to combine and allow to sit for 1 hour
5. After the hour, fine strain the zest and espresso beans out of your mixture (yields 16 ounces/about 10 cocktails)

Elixir

3200 16th Street
San Francisco, CA 94103
(415) 552-1633

elixirsf.com
cocktailclub@elixirsf.com

Established
1858

Leadership
H. Joseph, Ehrmann, Proprietor

The Petit Café

Inspired by the classic Irish Coffee, a drink made famous in San Francisco, this smaller, colder and bolder version is a sophisticated cocktail rich with botanicals and complimentary flavors.

Submitted by: H. Joseph Ehrmann, Elixir

Serve in a snifter (or small wine glass):
- 1 ½ ounces coffee liqueur (Galliano Ristretto preferred)
- 1 ½ ounces Green Chartreuse
- Heavy Cream
- Brown sugar

1. In a chilled container, whip the heavy cream to a thick consistency while retaining fluidity (We use a milk shake machine in the bar)
2. Separately, stir the first two ingredients in a mixing glass of ice for about 20 seconds
3. Strain into a snifter or small wine glass
4. Top with the whipped cream, floating it over the top of a bar spoon
5. Garnish with a pinch of brown sugar in the center

Establishment

1197 Peachtree N.E., Suite 517
Atlanta, GA 30361
(404) 347-5291

establishmentatlanta.com
info@establishmentatlanta.com

Established
2016

Leadership
Brandon Lewis and David Reed

Irish Alarm Clock

Submitted by: David Reed, Establishment Midtown

Serve in a short beer glass:
- 1 ounce Glendalough Irish Whiskey
- 4 ounces Guinness Stout
- 4 ounces Banjo Cold Brew Nitro Draft Coffee
1. Layer contents in sequence over ice in a short beer glass
2. Add simple syrup and/or Irish Cream or serve as is depending on individual taste

Full Throttle Saloon

12997 State Highway 34
Sturgis, SD 57785
(605) 423-4584

fullthrottlesaloon.com

Established
2016

Leadership
Jesse James Dupree
Michael Ballard

Oil Spill

The legendary Full Throttle Saloon returns bigger and better than ever in 2016 after a fire burned the original location in 2015. The Oil Spill incorporates their own coffee flavored moonshine known as "Saloonshine."

Submitted by: Full Throttle Saloon

Serve in a pilsner glass:
- 1 ½ ounces coffee flavored moonshine
- 3 ounces Guinness or chocolate stout beer
1. Pour beer over moonshine in glass and serve

Second bonus cocktail recipe from Full Thottle!
Bulldog Grin

Submitted by: Full Throttle Saloon

Serve in a rocks glass:
- 2 ounces coffee flavored moonshine
- 2 ounces skim milk
- 1 ½ ounces Coca-Cola
1. Shake over ice in a cocktail shaker
2. Strain into a rocks glass with ice

The Honeymoon

300 Main Street
Houston TX 77002
(281) 846-6995

thehoneymoonhtx.com
info@thehoneymoonhtx.com

Established
2014

Leadership
Charlotte Loreman, Brad Moore, Ryan Rouse & Matt Toomey

Coffee Mixology: The Honeymoon

Café du Monde

This cocktail pays homage to the famous café in New Orleans by the name and the fact it features the chicory coffee that they are known for. In a way, it's a nod to the bar side of the café at The Honeymoon, as well as to the coffee side. It also embraces the shared cultural history of our organization with the city of New Orleans.

Submitted by: Julie Lozano, The Honeymoon

Serve in a coupe:
- 1 ½ ounces Claude VS Cognac
- ½ ounce Zucca Rubarbaro Amaro
- 1 ounce chicory iced coffee
- ½ ounce simple syrup
1. Combine all ingredients in a mixing glass
2. Stir until condensation builds on the outside of the glass
3. Strain into a chilled coupe
4. Flame an orange peel and drop into the coupe for garnish

Mr. C's Irish Pub

1570 Dairy Ashford
Houston, TX 77077
(281) 497-8783

mrcsirishpub.com
ciaransimon@gmail.com

Established
2015

Leadership
Ciaran Simon, Owner

Squad Car Martini

Submitted by: Ciaran Simon, Mr. C's Irish Pub

Serve in a martini glass:
- 1 ½ ounces 360 Glazed Donut Vodka
- 2 ounces Starbucks Unsweetened Iced Coffee
- 2 ounces half and half
- ½ ounce simple syrup
1. Add all ingredients into a shaker with ice
2. Shake vigorously for 30 seconds
3. Strain into a martini glass

Piastra

45 W Park Square
Marietta, GA 30060
(770) 425-9300

piastrarestaurant.com
piastrarestaurant@gmail.com

Established
2015

Leadership
The Plates Restaurant LLC
Greg Lipman, Chef

Coffee Mixology: Piastra

Hazelnut Mint Chocolate Iced Espresso

Submitted by: Greg Lipman, Piastra

Serve in a tumbler:
- 1 ounce simple syrup
- 2 leaves fresh mint
- 1 tall shot espresso
- 2 ounces white rum
- 1 ounce Frangelico

1. Muddle mint in cocktail shaker
2. Add simple syrup
3. Add rum and Frangelico
4. Fill with ice and shake
5. Pour espresso into tumbler
6. Pour shaken drink over espresso

The Red Rabbit Kitchen and Bar

2718 J Street
Sacramento, CA 95816
(916) 706-2275

theredrabbit.net
matt@theredrabbit.net

Established
2013

Leadership
Matt Nurge, John Bays & Sonny Mayugba

A Black Deep V
Simple. Equal parts cocktail. Delicious.

Submitted by: Christopher Sinclair, The Red Rabbit

Serve in a rocks glass:
- 1 ounce bourbon
- 1 ounce Averna Liqueur
- 1 ounce cold brewed coffee
- 2 dashes orange bitters
1. Measure and pour all ingredients into mixing glass
2. Add ice
3. Stir & strain into a chilled cocktail glass
4. Garnish with orange swath

The Roosevelt Room

307 West 5th Street
Austin, TX 78701
(512) 609-8245

therooseveltroomatex.com
rooseveltroomatex@gmail.com

Leadership
Justin Lavenue and Dennis Gobis

Do You Even Lift?
The drink is based on one of the newest categories of mixed drinks, the Lift, created by Eric Adkins and Jennifer Colliau.

Submitted by: Justin Lavenue, The Roosevelt Room

Serve in an 8 ounce fizz glass:
- 1 ounce dark rum (El Dorado 5-year is perfect)
- ½ ounce coffee liqueur
- ½ ounce orgeat (almond syrup)
- ½ ounce cream
- 3-4 ounces of cream soda

1. Shake above (except the cream soda) well
2. Double-strain into a chilled fizz glass without ice
3. Top with cream soda (slowly poured 6 inches above the glass) until the foam "lifts" above the top of the glass
4. Garnish with Cayenne Pepper/Cinnamon powder blend
5. Serve with a large straw placed in the middle of the glass

Spenard Roadhouse

1049 W. Northern Lights Blvd.
Anchorage AK 99503
(907) 770-ROAD

spenardroadhouse.com

Established
2009

Leadership
Laile Fairbairn, Owner
Shawna Calt, Bar Manager

Devil's Breakfast

Submitted by: Lana Ramos, Spenard Roadhouse

Serve in a martini glass:
- 1 ounce Jim Beam Devil's Cut Bourbon
- ½ ounce Kahlua
- ½ ounce Frangelico
- ½ shot of espresso
- Orange zest
1. Add liquor to a mixing glass
2. Brew espresso on top of the liquor as to cool the espresso down as it pours
3. Add ice and shake with your preferred shaker vigorously Strain into cocktail glass
4. Zest an orange over the drink to capture all of the oils into the drink

Talbott Tavern

107 W. Stephen Foster Avenue
Bardstown, KY 40004
(502) 348-3494

talbotts.com
talbott@bardstown.com

Established
1779

"We are the original bourbon bar. We have served bourbon since bourbon and bars met."

Buffalo Coffee

This is a popular drink at the Talbott Tavern in the winter.

Submitted by: Old Talbott

Serve in a clear coffee glass:
- 6 ounces coffee
- 2 ounces Buffalo Trace Bourbon Cream
- Whipped cream
1. Pour coffee into in glass
2. Float bourbon cream on top
3. Add whipped cream on top of cream
4. Be sure to serve in a clear coffee glass, not a cup, so you can see the layer in the drink

Tavern Law

1406 12th Avenue
Seattle, WA 98125
(206) 719-8461

tavernlaw.com
michaelacadden@gmail.com

Established
2009

Leadership
Michael Cadden, General Manager/Bartender

The Treaty of Paris

(Notes by Michael Cadden) This cocktail takes your taste buds on a bit of a journey. It's salty then sweet, with a mild herbal bitter coffee finish. Think salted caramel only more depth. Well balanced with multiple layer of flavor.

Submitted by: Michael Cadden, Tavern Law

Serve in a champagne coupe:
- 1 ½ ounces Laird's Applejack bonded 100 proof
- ½ ounce Licor 43
- ½ ounce Green Chartreuse
- ½ ounce espresso
- 5 dashes Scrappy's Theo Chocolate Bitters
1. Combine all ingredients and shake with fresh, cold ice
2. Double strain through a hawthorn strainer then a fine mesh strainer into a cocktail coupe glass
3. Garnish with a dusting of fine grain Pink Himalayan salt

The Third Man

116 Avenue C
New York, NY 10003

thethirdmannyc.com

Established
2013

Leadership
Christian Daly, Manager

Pick Me Up

(Notes by Christian Daly) Below is one of my favorite coffee creations, the Pick Me Up. This cocktail is a strong and smooth espresso based drink featuring Solbeso, a brand new spirit made from the South American Cacao plant.

Submitted by: Christian Daly, The Third Man

Serve in a champagne coupe:
- 1 ½ ounce espresso infused Solbeso (recipe below)
- ½ ounce vanilla simple syrup
- ¾ ounce heavy cream
- 1 egg white
1. Shake ingredients and pour into a champagne coupe
2. Top with Ghirardelli 70% dark chocolate shavings

Solbeso Express Infusion
- Ground espresso
- 1 bottle of Solbeso
1. Fill ¼ of a quart bottle with espresso
2. Fill remaining quart with bottle of Solbeso
3. Let sit for 24 hours
4. Strain twice through fine strainer or once through milk cloth in to a fresh quart container

Trenchermen

2039 W. North Avenue
Chicago, IL 60647
(773) 661-1540

trenchermen.com
info@trenchermen.com

Established
2012

Leadership
Heisler Hospitality

Coffee Mixology: Trenchermen

Early & Often

The name Early & Often is twofold. Back in the shady days of Chicago politics (not like the upright and honest folks we have in office nowadays) citizens were encouraged to vote "early and often." Chicagoans also enjoy their cocktails often and their coffee early - so there ya go!

Submitted by: Nic Lutton, Trenchermen

Serve in a rocks glass:
- 1 ounce dark rum
- 1 ounce Salmiaki Dala Scandinavian Fernet
- ¼ ounce Rich Coffee Demerara Syrup
- 2 dashes orange bitters

1. Pour all ingredients in a mixing cup or cocktail shaker
2. Stir with ice and strain into a rocks glass with a large chunk of ice
3. Garnish with an expressed swath of orange peel

Vanguard Lounge

516 East Fremont Street
Las Vegas, NV 89101
(702) 868-7800

vanguardlv.com

Established
2010

Dram Good Coffee

Submitted by: Isaiah Thomas, Vanguard Lounge

Serve in a rocks glass:
- 1 ounce vanilla vodka
- 1 ½ ounces espresso
- 3 ounces Guinness
- ¼ ounce bitter truth pimento dram
- ¾ ounce condensed milk
1. Combine ingredients into mixing glass and stir
2. Serve in a rocks glass over ice

The Way Station

683 Washington Avenue
Brooklyn, NY 11238

tws.bar

Established
2011

Leadership
Andy Heidel, Proprietor

Coffee Mixology: The Way Station

Uhura's Kiss

The Star Trek episode, **Plato's Stepchildren**, featured the first interracial kiss on television. In it, Lieutenant Uhura and Captain Kirk shared a very controversial moment on American network television in 1968. This drink, Uhura's Kiss, celebrates this moment.

Submitted by: Andy Heidel and the staff and regulars of The Way Station

Serve in an espresso cup:
- 1 ounce Patron XO Café Tequilla
- 1 ounce Stoli Salted Karamel
- 1 lemon rind twist

1. Pour Stoli and Patron in a shaker filled with ice
2. Shake vigorously
3. Strain into espresso cup
4. Garnish with a twist of lemon

Bonus Coffee Cocktail: Saints+Sinners

675 Ponce de Leon Avenue Market N NE
Atlanta, Ga 30308
(404) 852-7023

1821bitters.com
drink@1821bitters.com

Established
2015

Leadership
Kristin Wingfield Koefod and Missy Koefod, Co-Owners

Saints+Sinners

Submitted by: Kristen Wingfield Koefod, 18.21 Bitters

Serve in a rocks glass:
- 2 ounces Rye Whiskey
- 1 ounce half and half
- ½ ounce 18.21 Coffee Vanilla Cocoa Syrup
- ½ ounce HooDoo Chicory Liqueur
- 10 drops 18.21 Barrel Aged Havana+Hide Bitters
1. Shake all ingredients with ice and strain into rocks glass over large cube (for a fun twist, use a coffee ice cube)
2. Garnish with a sprinkle of nutmeg

40 Steak and Seafood

1401 Interchange Avenue
Bismarck ND 58501
(701) 244-4040

40steakandseafood.com
dalezimmerman@gmail.com

Established
2014

Leadership
Dale and Melodie Zimmerman

Holiday Mule

40 Steak and Seafood specializes in whiskeys and bourbons and have over 150 different options available at any given time. With six fireplaces and a rustic cozy setting, it is the perfect setting for Christmas drinks.

Submitted by: Julia Redig, 40 Steak and Seafood

Serve in a copper mug:
- 1 ounce Jack Fire (cinnamon whiskey)
- ¾ ounce fresh lime juice
- Ginger beer

1. Combine Jack Fire and lime juice in a copper mug
2. Fill mug with crushed ice
3. Top off with ginger beer
4. Stir
5. Garnish with a lime wedge and a cinnamon stick

116 Crown

116 Crown Street
New Haven, CT 06510

116crown.com
info@116crown.com

Established
2007

Leadership
John & Danielle Ginnetti

116 CROWN

Red Hot Chocolate

Submitted by: John Ginnetti, 116 Crown

Serve in an Irish coffee mug:
- 1 ounce Campari
- 2 ounces brandy, preferably Germain-Robin
- 3 ounces whole milk
- 2 tablespoons chocolate chips (or equal amount crushed disks, accounting for volume differences) at least 55% cocoa, preferably DeBauve & Gallais

1. Put milk, cream & chocolate in a milk frothing cup used with espresso
2. Froth milk as you would for cappuccino
3. When milk is hot remove frothing wand and whisk or stir vigorously until chocolate is completely melted
4. Add Campari & brandy
5. Pour into mug and serve

Boiler Room

210 Broadway, Suite 90
Fargo, ND 58102
(701) 478-1990

info@boilerroomfargo.com
boilerroomfargo.com.com

Established
2014

Leadership
Dan Hurder & Christian D'Agostino, Co-Owners
Paul McMahon, General Manager

Fezziwig (a.k.a. The Fargo Fizz)

Submitted by: Davin Henrik, Mixologist at the Boiler Room

Serve in a collins glass:
- 1 egg white
- 2 ounces Old Tom Gin
- 1 ¾ ounces rhubarb infused elderflower liquor
- ¼ ounce lemon juice
- ¼ ounce lime juice
- ½ ounce simple syrup
- ¼ ounce heavy cream

1. Dry shake (no ice) all ingredients for 15 seconds
2. Add 5 ice chips and shake until you cannot hear the ice anymore
3. Strain into a collins glass, fill the glass with ginger ale, or lemon-lime soda
4. Stop pouring before the foam goes over the top of the glass
5. Pour ginger ale/soda around the inside of the shaker and wait from 30 seconds up to a minute and slow pour the soda into the glass

Butch McGuire's

20 West Division Street
Chicago, IL 60622
(312) 787-4318

butchmcguires.com

Established
1961

Leadership
Bobby McGuire, Owner
Justin Cordes, General Manager

Butch McGuire's holiday cheer!

Holiday Mixology: Butch McGuire's

Yuletide

In parts of Europe, a shot of Aquavit followed by a sip of strong, dark beer is considered tradition around the holidays. Butch McGuire's decided to spice it up a little by adding Irish Whiskey into the mix. The rich caraway and coriander aroma of the Aquavit will linger in the glass long after the liquid is gone, and is complimented well by a bold, rich winter Ale.

Submitted by: Matthew Czerwinski, Head Bartender

Serve in a champagne flute:
- 1 ½ ounces Tullamore D.E.W. Irish Whiskey
- ½ ounce North Shore Aquavit Private Reserve (or similar Aquavit)
- ½ ounce simple syrup
- 4 ounces Deschutes Jubelale (or any dark, spiced winter ale)

1. Create a spice blend of equal parts brown sugar, cinnamon, and nutmeg
2. Pour the Aquavit into a champagne flute
3. Swirl to rinse the flute with Aquavit, then discard the liquid
4. Rim the lip of the flute with the spice blend (a little moisture will make the spices adhere to the glass)
5. Build the drink with the simple syrup, whiskey and ale, finishing with the ale to give the drink a nice frothy head

Cardinal Tavern

901 South Clinton Street
Baltimore, MD 21221
(410) 327-7850

cardinaltav.com

Leadership
Justin Hostetter & Lindsey Porreca, Co-Owners
Steven Grant, Executive Chef

Green Christmas Mule

Submitted by: Cardinal Tavern

Serve in a copper mug:
- Cilantro & jalapeno
- 1 ½ ounces Ketel One Vodka
- ½ ounce triple sec
- ½ ounce Freshly squeezed lime juice
- ½ ounce ginger liqueur
- Ginger beer

1. Muddle cilantro and jalapeno in mug
2. Add all other ingredients other than ginger beer
3. Fill with crushed ice
4. Top off glass with ginger beer
5. Garnish with a jalapeno slice and a sprig of cilantro

Dickie Brennan's Steakhouse

716 Iberville Street
New Orleans, LA 70130
(504) 522-2467

dickiebrennanssteakhouse.com

Established
1998

Leadership
Dickie Brennan, Steve Pettus and Lauren Brennan Brower

Réveillon Revelry

This cocktail captures the spirit of réveillon, the French celebration of a long dinner on the day before Christmas Day and New Year's Day.

Submitted by: Dickie Brennan's Steakhouse

Serve in a pilsner glass:
- 1 ½ ounces of Maker's Mark Bourbon
- ½ ounce amaretto
- ½ ounce Steen's Cane Syrup
- 2 dashes of El Guapo Chicory-Pecan Bitters
- Lazy Magnolia's Southern Pecan Nut Brown Ale
1. Combine first four ingredients in a shaker
2. Add ice and shake
3. Strain into a pilsner glass
4. Top with beer and stir

Herbie's Vintage 72

405 North Euclid
St. Louis, MO 63108
(314) 769-9595

herbies.com
amanda@herbies.com

Established
2008

Leadership
Aaron Teitelbaum, owner

Sugar Plum

Submitted by: Amanda Wilgus, Bar Manager, Herbie's Vintage 72

Serve in a snifter:
- 1 ½ ounces Pearl Plum
- ½ ounce Dolin Blanc
- ½ ounce Velvet Fallernum
- ½ ounce lemon juice
1. Combine all ingredients into a shaker
2. Shake and strain into snifter
3. Garnish with a lemon twist

Novela

662 Mission Street
San Francisco, CA 94105

novelasf.com
info@novelasf.com

Established
2013

Leadership
John Park, Owner
Suzanne Miller, General Manager
Suzie Robinson, Assistant General Manager

Hot Buttered Bourbon

Submitted by: Suzanne Miller, Novela

Serve in an Irish coffee mug:
- 2 ounces butter-fat washed and spiced bourbon whiskey
- 3 – 4 ounces hot water
- Amaretto whipped cream
1. Pour buttered bourbon into mug and top off with hot water
2. Add amaretto whipped cream to the top and serve

Butter Bourbon Recipe
1. In a medium saucepan, melt one stick of unsalted butter with one tablespoon of packaged pumpkin-pie spice blend over low heat
2. Place into gallon-sized mason jar, and slowly add in 750 ml Maker's Mark (or another sweet bourbon)
3. Combine well, and place into freezer overnight
4. The fat will separate and float to the top, leaving only butter flavor and spice behind
5. Remove fat and use whiskey

Amaretto Whipped Cream Recipe
1. Combine one pint heavy whipping cream with 2 ounces Amaretto and whip as normal

The Royal Mile

210 4th Street
Des Moines, IA 50309
(515) 280-3771

royalmilebar.com
info@royalmilebar.com

Established
2001

Leadership
Full Court Press, ownership group
Kathleen Kelly, General Manager
Sean Courtney, Bar Manager

Cedar Ridge Mulled Cider

The Mary's Mulled Cider is named for the bar manager's mother. It's actually a variant of her recipe.

Mulled cider evolved from wassail, a beverage drunk in medieval Germany and the apple producing areas of southern England at Yuletide to guarantee a good apple harvest next year.

Nearly any spirit would work in this cocktail, it can be fun to play around with different flavor combinations. We like to use the local stuff from Cedar Ridge here in Iowa.

Submitted by: Sean Courtney, Bar Manager, the Royal Mile

Serve in an Irish coffee mug:
- 1 ½ ounce Cedar Ridge Bourbon
- 6 ounces Mary's Mulled Cider (recipe below)
- 1 cinnamon stick
1. In an Irish coffee mug pour bourbon and fill with Mary's Apple Cider
2. Garnish with a cinnamon stick

Mary's Mulled Cider Recipe:
- 1 jug apple cider (non-alcoholic)
- 1 whole orange
- 20-30 clove buds
- 3 green cardamom seeds
- 3 cinnamon sticks
- 3 cassia sticks
- 4 coriander seeds
- 3 pods star anise

Mary's Mulled Cider Recipe (continued):
1. In a preheated crock pot set to high (make sure that your slow cooker is big enough to hold your cider), toast the cardamom, cinnamon, cassia star anise and coriander
2. Jam the clove buds into the orange, distributing evenly
3. When you start to smell the spices, add all ingredients other ingredients to the slow cooker
4. Turn to low and let simmer for about 2 hours
5. After 2 hours remove the orange with the cloves in it and discard
6. Turn the slow cooker to warm, and serve

Sloppy Joe's

201 Duval Street
Key West, FL 33040
(305) 294-5715

sloppyjoes.com

Established
Located at the Corner of Duval and Greene Since 1937

Leadership
Chris Mullins, CEO

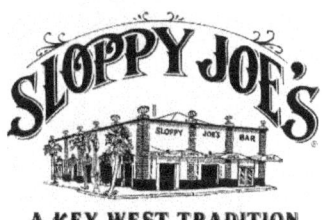

Snow Daze

You don't have to have snow outside to get into the Christmas spirit when you are enjoying Sloppy Joe's Snow Daze cocktail!

Submitted by: Sloppy Joe's staff

Serve in a cocktail glass:
- 1/2 ounce bourbon
- 1/2 ounce RumChata
- 1/2 ounce butter shot
- 1 ounces cream
1. Combine all ingredients in a blender
2. Blend with ice
3. Pour into glass
4. Sprinkle with nutmeg and garnish with mint leaf

Supply and Demand

3223 Cains Hill Drive NW
Atlanta, GA 30305
(404) 863-1651

supplydemandatl.com

Established
2015

Leadership
Brandon Lewis and Dave Reed

Holiday Mixology: Supply and Demand

The Mistlefoot

Supply and Demand is a speakeasy open to members only. Membership is free, but you must be an approved member to enjoy this cocktail, and any others, at Supply and Demand.

Submitted by: Albro Vrooman, Supply and Demand

Serve in a chilled coupe:
- 1 ½ ounces bourbon
- 1 ounce Meletti Cioccolato
- 1/4 ounce Yellow Chartreuse
- 3 dashes Xocolatl Mole Bitters
- 3 dashes Regan's Orange Bitters
- 1 ounce orange juice
- Bourbon whipped cream
- One halved cinnamon stick

1. Orange zest a chilled coupe cocktail glass
2. Add the rest of the ingredients into a cocktail shaker and shake with ice
3. Double strain into the chilled/zested coupe
4. Top with bourbon whip cream and finish with cinnamon stick and more orange zest

Urban Tree Cidery

1465 Howell Mill Road NW
Atlanta, GA 30318
(404) 855-5546

urbantreecidery.com
info@urbantreecidery.com

Established
2016

Leadership
Maria and Tim Resuta

Lenox Park

The Lenox Park will elevate your holiday palate. The Bar Chef's (drinkable vinegar mixers) Apple Sage Shrub provides an earthy sweetness that is perfectly balanced by Urban Tree's Barrel Aged cider. American Spirit Whiskey wakes up those sleepy taste buds and the splash of Sparkling Cranberry juice complements each element of the cocktail. The Lenox Park will save you from your soon coming food coma.

Submitted by: Jessica D. Smith, Mixologist (@TheBarChefShrub)

Serve in a stemless wine glass:
- 1 ounce Apple Sage Shrub (suggested: TheBarChefShrub)
- 2 ounces American Spirit Whiskey
- 2 ounces Urban Tree Cidery Barrel Aged Cider
- Splash of Sparkling Cranberry Juice
- Red Apple slice and a single mint leaf for garnish

1. Fill a stemless wine glass with ice
2. In a shaker, add ice plus the first two ingredients
3. Shake vigorously for 20-30 seconds
4. Strain the mixture into prepared wine glass
5. Fill glass with Barrel Aged Cider
6. Splash with Sparkling Cranberry juice
7. Garnish with thinly sliced red apple and single mint leaf

Whiskey Bar

788 N. Jackson Street
Milwaukee, WI 53202

whiskeybarmilwaukee.com

Established
2009

Leadership
Ben Richardson, General Manager

Holiday Honey Hot Toddy

Submitted by: Ben Richardson, General Manager

Serve in an Irish coffee mug:
- 2 ounces Bushmills Irish Honey Whiskey
- 1 ounce fresh honey
- 1 cinnamon stick
- 1 lemon wedge with cloves pressed into it
1. Fill all ingredients in a mug and add steaming hot water
2. Stir and serve

Bonus Holiday Cocktail: The Bitter Grinch

675 Ponce de Leon Ave Market N NE
Atlanta, GA 30308
(404) 852-7023

1821bitters.com
drink@1821bitters.com

Established
2015

Leadership
Kristin Wingfield Koefod and Missy Koefod, Co-Owners

Holiday Mixology: 18.21 Bitters

The Bitter Grinch

Submitted by: Kristen Wingfield Koefod, 18.21 Bitters

Serve in a coupe:
- 1 ½ ounces Mezcal
- ½ ounce 18.21 Lemon Basil Syrup
- ½ ounce Yellow Chartreuse
- ½ ounce lime juice
- 1 egg white
- Absinthe
- Sea salt

1. Shake all ingredients in a cocktail shaker vigorously without ice
2. Add ice and shake again for 10-15 seconds
3. Rinse the coupe with absinthe, then strain cocktail into glass
4. Garnish with a green leaf and a sprinkle of sea salt

Author's Notes/Resources

I encourage you to learn more about these businesses and what makes them so special. To make your job a little easier, here's a combined recap of the websites for both **Coffee Mixology** and **Holiday Mixology**:

18.21 Bitters – *1821bitters.com*

40 Steak and Seafood – *40steakandseafood.com*

116 Crown – *116crown.com*

Boiler Room – *boilerroomfargo.com*

The Brooklynite – *brooklynitesa.com*

Buffalo Proper – *buffaloproper.com*

Butch McGuire's – *butchmcguires.com*

Cardinal Tavern – *cardinaltav.com*

Coffee House Cafe – *coffeehousecafe.com*

Dandelion Market – *dandelionmarketcharlotte.com*

Dickie Brenna's Steakhouse – *dickiebrennassteakhouse.com*

Elixir – *elixirsf.com*

Establishment - *establishmentatlanta.com*

Full Throttle Salooon – *fullthrottlesaloon.com*

Herbie's Vintage 72 – *herbies.com*

The Honeymoon – *thehoneymoonhtx.com*

Mr. C's Irish Pub – *mrcsirishpub.com*

Novela – *novelasf.com*

Piastra – *piastrarestaurant.com*

The Red Rabbit Kitchen and Bar – *redrabbit.net*

The Roosevelt Room – *therooseveltroomatx.com*

The Royal Mile – *royalmilebar.com*

Sloppy Joe's – *sloppyjoes.com*

Spenard Roadhouse – *spenardroadhouse.com*

Supply and Demand – *supplydemandatl.com*

Talbott Tavern – *talbotts.com*

Tavern Law – *tavernlaw.com*

The Third Man – *thethirdmannyc.com*

Trenchermen – *trenchermen.com*

Urban Tree Cidery – *urbantreecidery.com*

Vanguard Lounge – *vanguardlv.com*

The Way Station – *tws.bar*

Whiskey Bar – *whiskeybarmilwaukee.com*

Steve's Other Works

Small Brand America
Special Bourbon Edition

In ***Small Brand America V***, author Steve Akley explores small companies making a name for themselves with a truly American original: bourbon. Each has a little bit of a different take on making America's favorite distilled spirit. Inevitably, you will find yourself wanting to learn more about the companies and a desire to try their product(s).

Bourbon Mixology Series

Steve has published three books in his Bourbon Mixology series. The first shares cocktails from bourbon distilleries featured in Steve's book **Small Brand America V: Special Bourbon Edition** and the follow-ups feature signature bourbon cocktails from iconic bars.

Special Thanks

To my sister-in-law Lee Ann Sciuto and my wife Amy, for their help in editing this book.

Thanks to my daughter Cat for just being herself.

Hats off to Mark Hansen (*mappersmark@gmail.com*) for the great cover design. He's the greatest graphic artist you will ever find!

The following individuals from the featured companies not only couldn't have been nicer, without their help this book would not have been possible:
Andy Heidel/The Way Station, Christian Daly/The Third Man, Michael Cadden/Tavern Law, H. Joseph Ehrmann/Elixir, Pam/Talbott Tavern, Matt Nurge/The Red Rabbit, Justin Lavenue/The Roosevelt Room, Catharine Buck/Dandelion Market, Jon Karel/Buffalo Proper, Lana Ramos/Spenard Roadhouse, Jeret Peña/The Brooklynite, Evan/Full Throttle Saloon, Dillon/Vanguard Lounge, Christopher Crowe/The Honeymoon Café and Bar, Mary Doyle/Heisler Hospitality, Nic Lutton/Trenchermen, Heather Carmichael/Coffee House Cafe, Wesley Noble/Dickie Brennan's Steakhouse, Donna Edwards/Sloppy Joe's, Dale Zimmerman/40 Steak and Seafood, Amanda Wilgus/Herbie's Vintage 72, Matt Czerwinski/Butch McGuire's Tavern and Grill, Lindsey Porreca/Cardinal Tavern, Sarah Feinauer/Whiskey Bar, Davin Henrik/Boiler Room, John Ginnetti/116 Crown & Suzanne Miller/Novela, Kitsy Rose/Kitsy Rose PR.

Lastly, lots of love for my father, Larry Akley. He's always with us in spirit.

Love A Cat Charity – Honolulu, Hawai'i

Steve Akley proudly supports the mission of Love A Cat Charity with a donation of a portion of the proceeds of the sale of all of his books.

Mission Statement

Love A Cat Charity's mission is to help end euthanasia of unwanted cats by caring for feral and abandoned felines, spaying or neutering them and, when appropriate, adopting them out. Love A Cat Charity emphasizes the use of Trap-Neuter-Return (TNR) technique to humanely control feral cat populations. Cats are humanely trapped, spayed or neutered and returned to their outdoor homes. TNR improves the cats' health and stabilizes the colony while allowing them to live out their lives outdoors. No new kittens are born and the cats no longer experience the stresses of mating and pregnancy.

Support of Love A Cat Charity in Honolulu, HI, helps cats like this sweet kitty

Love A Cat Charity
P.O. Box 11753
Honolulu, HI 96828
loveacatcharity.org

About the Author

Steve today and as a grade schooler meeting Andre the Giant

Steve Akley is a lifelong St. Louis resident. His approach to writing is very simple. He knows his passion comes from topics he enjoys so he sticks to what he knows best. He maintains an author's page on Amazon.com. Just search his name on the site.

He can be reached via email: info@steveakley.com.

Find Steve on Social Media

 & @steveakley & Steve Akley

Bourbon Zeppelin & The Bourbon Show

Steve has two new projects for bourbon fans. The first is a monthly newsletter called **Bourbon Zeppelin** that contains news about "all things bourbon." The second is a podcast called **The Bourbon Show** featuring bourbon talk, guests, news and tastings. Find out more by logging onto Steve's websites:

steveakley.com & ABVNetwork.com

www.ingramcontent.com/pod-product-compliance
Lightning Source LLC
Chambersburg PA
CBHW031456040426
42444CB00007B/1122